Brave from the Inside Out™
My Body, My Voice

by
Candace Johnson

Character designs for Tad and Blossom by
Zachary Coomes

Covered in Grace Books

Brave from the Inside Out™: My Body, My Voice
Text © 2025 Candace Johnson
Character designs for Tad and Blossom © 2025 Zachary Coomes
Illustrations © 2025 Candace Johnson

All rights reserved. No part of this book may be reproduced, stored in a retrieval system, or transmitted in any form or by any means—electronic, mechanical, photocopying, recording, or otherwise—without prior written permission from the publisher, except in the case of brief quotations used in reviews, articles, or educational materials.

Published by Covered in Grace Books
ISBN: 979-8-9999292-04
Library of Congress Control Number: 2025918801

Printed in the United States of America

Scripture quotations are taken from the Holy Bible, New International Version®, NIV®.
Copyright © 1973, 1978, 1984, 2011 by Biblica, Inc.™ Used by permission.
All rights reserved worldwide.
For more resources, visit: www.coveredingracebooks.com

For every child God calls brave, and for the grown-ups called to protect them. With love and gratitude to my family for their support.

Violet stood beneath the blossom tree, her toes curling in the cool grass as she sang, "Jesus loves the little children..." Above, a cocoon swayed in the breeze — quiet, still, waiting. In the pond, a tadpole hid beneath a lily pad — quiet, listening, waiting. Across the pond, a boy paused mid-rock skip. He knew that melody.

As he walked through the tall grass, he hummed the next line under his breath—"Red and yellow, black and white... they are precious in His sight..." Violet turned. They looked at each other, then smiled—and sang the last line together, soft and sure: "Jesus loves the little children of the world."

As their voices joined together, something began to change. The cocoon above Violet quivered—just a little at first. Then, with a soft crackle, a glow peeked through the threads. Tiny wings unfolded, bright and shimmering. At the same time, in the pond nearby, the tadpole gave a little wiggle. Then another. His tail shrank, and his legs began to stretch. He blinked, surprised—a frog now, where once a tadpole floated and waited.

She paused, then said, "Hi… my name is Violet." Kristian smiled wider. "Nice to meet you, Violet. I'm Kristian." They stood quietly for a moment. "I sing it," Violet said softly, "when I want to feel better inside." Just then, a gentle voice came from above. "And that's a very brave song to sing," said the voice.

Violet gasped. "Did you hear that?" Kristian's eyes widened. "Who said that?" From behind a leaf, a glowing butterfly stepped into view. "I did," she said kindly. "Hi... my name is Blossom." Kristian looked at Violet. "Did that butterfly just talk?" Violet nodded slowly. "Yes... she did. And she's so beautiful."

Blossom fluttered gently. "I loved hearing you sing that song," she said. Violet looked up. "Wait… how do you know that song?" Kristian added, "Yeah—how do you know it?" Blossom just smiled.

From the pond nearby, a small voice spoke up. "We all know that song," it said. "All God's creatures do." Violet's eyes grew wide. "D-d-did that f-f-frog just talk?" Kristian's smile stretched across his face. "Yes, he did! And that's so cool!"

The frog gave a friendly hop forward. "My name's Tad," he said with a proud little puff of his chest. Tad tilted his head. "That is a very brave song to sing." Kristian looked curious. "Why does that song make you brave?"

Tad leaned in gently. "Can I tell you something really important?" The children nodded. Tad's eyes softened. "Bravery isn't about never being scared," he said. "It's about listening to that feeling in your stomach and speaking up when something doesn't feel right."

"That feeling inside your stomach?" Kristian asked. "That's your stomach voice," Tad explained. "It's your body's way of saying, 'Pay attention—something is wrong.' It's there to protect you."

Blossom's wings glowed softly. "Your stomach voice can feel twisty or icky when something doesn't feel safe," she added. Kristian and Violet looked at each other. "But how do we know what it's trying to say?" Violet asked.

Blossom's wings sparkled as she spoke softly. "Your stomach voice speaks up when something feels wrong—like if someone tries to tickle you and you don't want them to." Kristian's eyes widened. "Even if they say it's just a joke?" Tad nodded. "Yes. If it doesn't feel right to you, it's okay to say no."

"Your stomach voice helps you know when something isn't safe—no matter what someone else says," Tad continued. Blossom added, "Like if a grown-up tells you to keep a secret that makes you feel scared or weird inside." "Or if someone touches your body in a way you don't like," Tad said.

"Even if they say it's just a game... or even if they say you'll get in trouble for telling." Blossom's wings glowed gently. "Remember to always use your voice," she said. "And say No."

Violet looked down at her hands. "But... what if I'm scared to say no?" Kristian whispered, "Yeah... what if I don't feel brave?" Blossom fluttered gently in front of them. "Being brave doesn't always feel big or loud," she said.

"Sometimes being brave means listening to your stomach voice and speaking up anyway." Tad hopped closer to Kristian. "You are always allowed to say no," he said. "Even if it's someone older. Even if they say you'll get in trouble. Even if it's someone you love."

Violet and Kristian looked at each other. They weren't sure they felt brave— but something inside them wanted to be. Brave from the inside out.

Kristian looked up. "But what do we do when our stomach voice tells us something is wrong?" Blossom flew a little closer. "There are three things you can do," she said. "Say no, get away, and tell a safe grown-up."

Kristian raised his hand. "But how do we know who a safe grown-up is?" Tad said, "A safe grown-up—or a safe person—is someone who helps you, listens to you, and never makes you keep secrets that feel wrong."

Blossom added, "They believe you. They protect you. They listen with their hearts. And they never make you feel scared, confused, or hurt." Violet thought for a second. "Like… someone who lets me talk about my feelings, even if I'm crying or I don't know the right words to say.

Blossom nodded, glowing gently. "Yes, little one. Your safe person makes you feel calm and cared for. They never blame you for being honest — and they never hurt you." Tad grinned. Kristian smiled just a little. "I think I know who my safe person is."

Blossom came in a little closer. "Let's pretend for a moment — just to practice." Tad leaned in. "Let's say someone tries to tickle you, and your stomach voice says, No, I don't like that. What could you do?"

Violet stood a little taller. "I would say, No, stop! Then I'd move away." Kristian finished her sentence. "And I'd tell my safe person what happened." Blossom beamed. "Exactly. You listened to your stomach voice. You spoke up, and you asked for help. That's being brave. Brave from the inside out."

Violet took a deep breath. "It feels good to know what to do." Kristian nodded. "And it feels even better knowing I'm allowed to do it."

Violet looked down again. "What if I didn't say no?" she whispered. "What if I froze and couldn't do anything?" Blossom's glow softened. She flew close and looked Violet right in her eyes. "Listen closely, little one… It's not your fault."

Blossom nodded. "You are not bad. You are not to blame. And you are not alone." Kristian's voice was barely a whisper. "But... what if they said it was my fault?" Blossom shook her head. "They were wrong. No one is ever allowed to hurt you — and it is never your fault when they do."

Kristian sat up a little taller. "I don't ever want to make someone feel afraid. I want to be a safe person too." Blossom smiled gently. "That's what brave kids do. They protect themselves — and each other." Blossom circled around them slowly. "And there's something else that's very important," she said. "I want you both to know."

Violet and Kristian looked up. Tad moved in a little closer. "Just like no one is allowed to hurt you… you're not allowed to hurt others either." Blossom landed softly between them. "Hands are meant for helping, not hurting. That means no hitting, no pushing, and no touching someone's body in a way that makes them feel upset or unsafe."

Violet asked, "Even if I think it's just playing?" Tad nodded. "Yes. If someone says stop, you stop."

Blossom fluttered above their heads and smiled. "Now let's remember everything we've learned." Tad did a backflip and said, "Say it with us! Say it loud." Kristian stood tall. "My body belongs to me."

Violet nodded. "And I'm allowed to say no." Kristian added, "My body, my voice." Violet continued, "I can tell a safe person." Kristian added, "Even if someone is older." Violet continued, "Even if they say it's a secret."

Blossom's wings glowed one last time. "Because brave doesn't always roar — sometimes brave is a whisper that says, This is not okay."

Blossom smiled. "Yes, He did. He gave you a voice. He gave you wisdom. And He gave you the strength to speak up — even when it's hard." Tad gently added, "You are never too small to be brave…"

The sun dipped low, and Violet and Kristian whispered one last time: "My body. My voice. And I am brave from the inside out."

EVERY BODY IS BRAVE

Some kids walk. Some kids roll.
Some kids use signs, pictures, or devices to talk.
Some kids need extra help to move, learn, or feel calm.

Every child is different. Every child is important.
And every child deserves to feel safe, strong, and seen.

⭐ God made each of us—
one-of-a-kind—on purpose,
for a purpose.

Your differences are not mistakes.
They're part of the beautiful
way you were created.

Your body is yours.
Your voice matters.

And you are NEVER too small
or too different to be brave.

The sun dipped low, and Violet and Kristian whispered one last time: "My body. My voice. And I am brave from the inside out."

EVERY BODY IS BRAVE

Some kids walk. Some kids roll.
Some kids use signs, pictures, or devices to talk.
Some kids need extra help to move, learn, or feel calm.

Every child is different. Every child is important.
And every child deserves to feel safe, strong, and seen.

⭐ **God made each of us—
one-of-a-kind—on purpose,
for a purpose.**

Your differences are not mistakes.
They're part of the beautiful
way you were created.

**Your body is yours.
Your voice matters.**

**And you are NEVER too small
or too different to be brave.**

⭐ BRAVE AFFIRMATIONS ⭐

Say these out loud or in your heart every day.

- I can say no.

- My body, my voice.

- I can tell a safe person.

- Even if someone is older.

- Even if they say it's a secret

- My voice matters.

- I am strong on the inside and out.

- God is always with me.

Leap into courage

Shine bright, you are brave.

Bravery Certificate

You are brave, loved, and wonderfully made.

This certificate is awarded to:

_____

For showing bravery on:

_____

Signed:

"Be strong and courageous… for the Lord your God goes with you."

– Deuteronormy 31:6

Safety Numbers

In case of crisis or concern, these national hotlines are available 24/7:

→ National Sexual Assault Hotline (RAINN): 1-800-656–HOPE (4673)

→ National Human Trafficking Hotline: 1-888-373-7888 or text "BeFree" (233733)

→ National Runaway Safeline: 1-800-786-2929 (1-800-RUNAWAY)

→ National Domestic Violence Hotline: 1-800-799-SAFE (7233)

In any emergency, call: 911

✏️ Local Safety Contacts (Write in your area's numbers)

National Center for Missing & Exploited Children (CyberTipline): 1-800-843-5678 _____

Local Child Protective Services: _____

Safe School Contact or Counselor: _____

Local Police (non-emergency): _____

Other trusted local resource: _____

When a Child Speaks Up

If a child shares something that makes you pause. *Pause. Listen closely.*

Disclosures about unsafe touch or unsafe secrets may not come out in a single sentence — they may come in pieces, through questions, or even through play.

- **Take a deep breath and stay calm.**
- **Do not interrupt — let them speak in their own way.**
- **Believe them.**
- **Thank them for trusting you.**
- **Assure them they did the right thing.**
- **Seek help from the proper authorities.**

✨ *Studies confirm it matters. Supportive adult reactions reduce trauma symptoms and shorten recovery time. Negative or dismissive responses can have long-term harm.(Elliott & Briere, 1994; Ullman, 2007; Jonzon & Lindblad, 2004; NCTSN)."*

Your response matters. When children are heard and supported, they are **safer**, **stronger**, and **braver**.

A Message to Grown-Ups

Brave from the Inside Out™: My Body, My Voice is more than a story—it is a prevention tool and a movement to protect children. This book was designed for use in classrooms, counseling offices, medical practices, libraries, and homes. Its purpose is to raise awareness, spark conversations, and give children the language and confidence to speak up, set boundaries, and know they are never alone.

This book also includes a dedicated page acknowledging children with disabilities, affirming that their bodies and voices are equally valuable. Every child deserves the confidence to be heard and protected.

We encourage you to revisit this book often. Repetition builds trust, and trust opens the door for disclosure, healing, and safety. Thank you for joining us in this mission to empower children with courage from the inside out.

"Train up a child in the way he should go;
even when he is old he will not depart from it."
— Proverbs 22:6

Brave from the Inside Out™ Series

Created by Candace Johnson, Brave from the Inside Out™ is a faith-based series designed to help children understand emotions, safety, bravery, and belonging—one story at a time.

This Book:
My Body, My Voice
A story about body safety, personal boundaries, and using your voice.

Coming Soon:
My Voice, My Actions
A story about bullying, kindness, and standing up for yourself and others.

Brave in Every Emotion
A story about feelings, big emotions, and being brave in every mood.

My Way Is Brave Too
A story that celebrates disability, neurodiversity, and being uniquely you.

Join the Brave club

For updates and resources, visit:
www.coveredingracebooks.com